Ham Radio:

THE GENERAL LICENSE GUIDE TO UNDERSTAND EQUIPMENT AND BECOME A RADIO AMATEUR THE FAST AND EASY WAY

Descrierea CIP a Bibliotecii Naționale a României
BARRON, CRAIG
  Ham Radio : the general license guide to understand equipment and become a radio amateur the fast and easy way / by Craig Barron. - București : My Ebook, 2018
  ISBN 978-606-983-612-5
  654.195.6

HAM RADIO:

THE GENERAL LICENSE GUIDE TO UNDERSTAND EQUIPMENT AND BECOME A RADIO AMATEUR THE FAST AND EASY WAY

My Ebook Publishing House
Bucharest, 2018

CONTENTS

Chapter 1. **What is Ham Radio?**............................. 9
Chapter 2. **Transmitting Licences** 18
Chapter 3. **Equipment** 27
Chapter 4. **How to become a Radio Amateur** 40
Conclusion 53

INTRODUCTION

I want to thank you and congratulate you for buying the book, *"Ham Radio: The General License Guide To Understand Equipment And Become A Radio Amateur The Fast And Easy Way."*

This book contains proven steps and strategies on how to start your Ham Radio and get a license to operate your radio. You will get to know about tuning to the right frequency, when to tune and making consistent contacts by going through this book.

Thanks again for purchasing this book, I hope you enjoy it!

Chapter One
WHAT IS HAM RADIO?

Amateur Radio, also known as ham radio is generally a hobby and service which most people are interested in. Thousands of US citizens and also citizens of various countries across the world currently are making use of the ham radio. Using the Ham radio is fun, exciting, educative, and can be a source of help during emergency. It connects electronics, people and communication bringing them together. Ham radio has been used for communication ranging from across town, around the world and even into space.

It doesn't require internet access or even a mobile phone. People who use the ham radio are known as hams.

Ham radio was introduced within the last century, it has evolved in diverse ways and has grown into large community hosting licensed hams. Hams are everywhere connecting to the airwaves and constantly innovating several methods for improving the ham radio experience. Ham radios are made for everybody; it doesn't matter if you are in preschool or if you are a nerdy graduate. It is as attractive to a novice as it is to an expert in the field of technology.

Communication using the amateur radio relies on a wide range of frequency types, different antennas as well as radios. With the ham radio and also the absence of internet users can connect freely across the globe.

Ham radios have a variety of functions; it can be used for personal satisfaction and all-round communications including emergencies. They can also be used to understand the technique used in radios and its equipment. Computers, microphones, lasers, Morse keys, cameras, and their satellites are used to aid communication.

Hams may contact each other on air or even directly in person. Hams have clubs and organizations where people of like minds meet to strategize how to achieve conceived ideas and to mentor upcoming hams. From time to time they host conventions and meet-ups. Prior to the licensing of radios, hams less than seven years of using amateur radio as well as those with years of experience have been considered as hams. Becoming a ham requires nothing more than a passion for radio that will reflect in diverse ways. Not all hams you see have a good technical knowledge. Some do while others do not. There are no specific locations where ham radios thrive best, anywhere is perfect for a ham station.

Operating a ham radio s fun and most people s interest in amateur radios are driven by the fun aspect of it. Asides the excitement, Amateur radio could be very helpful in emergency situations especially when other services are unavailable. A typical example of an emergency case is the 1992 Hurricane Andrew that hit South Florida. It destroyed the common means of communication, its antennas, utility grid, and its cellular networks were all destroyed leaving victims almost helpless. At that time, amateur radio was the only source of communication and some payphones that were connected with underground lines. They are also used for other community services

Radio Amateurs also provide a valuable community service.

Amateur radio operators because of their several inventions and discoveries are called technical innovators. They have also contributed to the advanced modern technology.

Space travelers and astronaut use ham radios to link up with people when they are away from the earth. Amateur radios are very useful even on space.

The advantages of Amateur radio are very much while using the ham radio, it is easier to grasp the idea behind electronics. You get to meet new people, learn new languages, and improve your knowledge about the different parts of the world.

The field of Amateur radio is very broad having different areas where people can specialize in. You may decide to focus on building a new transceiver, an aerial dish or perhaps be connecting with rare DX countries using the short waves.

Some amateurs find the technical part of ham radio more interesting, so instead of using the ham radio, they build equipment, test available antennas for hams. They are not always available on air, except for cases where they want to do an assessment of their latest project or perhaps need to share an idea with someone on air.

Transmitting modes and Frequencies.

Hams use different frequencies type for communications. Anyone one with a radio scanner or receivers will be able to use the frequencies allocated by the FCC.

Most people are concerned about how to know the different stations, how to tune in to these stations. They will get to know that ham radios are not like the regular radios where you need channel numbers or assign a specific frequency to a station.

It is easier to create and keep communications ongoing with the ham radio, irrespective of the circumstances encountered during communication. That's how flexible it can be, but this can be a drawback as it will be difficult to make contact with a station because of the unavailability of a specific frequency.

However, there is a solution to this, and this involves operating within the range of gigahertz; starting at a little above the AM broadcast band to the microwave region. You can locate hams easily on frequency from above 1.6MHz (radio band) with wavelengths of about 160 meters to just above 27MHz (citizens band) having wavelengths as small as in millimeters. They are collectively known as shortwave bands or short-wave radios. For long distance communications at night, tune in to 1.6-15MHz while during the day for long-distance communication 15-27MHz.

Frequencies which FM radio uses hardly transmits signals to a distance farther than 50 miles, shortwaves from the ionosphere go directly from the transmitter to the antenna of the receiver.

Hams either use voices, Radio Teleprinter (RTTY), Morse keys and other modes for communication and making contacts. Morse code signals are often more efficient and reliable than voices. If voice transmissions are not getting through then, you should consider using Morse codes. Radio modems are also used by ham radio operators to communicate in different networks.

Chapter Two

TRANSMITTING LICENCE

Transmitting using frequencies or the amateur band can only be done with a license issued by the FCC. For training in all forms of radio communication, most countries require that the individual be issued a License. Listening to ham transmissions do not require a license. Everyone is free to do so.

All the Amateur Service located in different service are licensed services. Before license is given, the application to begin transmission has to be signed and approved by a government agency. Regulation and licensing are now a little difficult because equipment for hams and now easy to find and very much available for sale. It is important to license because amateurs can communicate without any of their activities being regulated, both locally and internationally.

The scope and power of the amateur radio is so wide and should not be too limited. So as not to prevent them from coexisting with other radio services.

Transmitting license regulations differ from country to country, but they all have something in common. Irrespective of the country you reside, you have to pass an examination before you will be issued a license. Details about this exam, materials, and tutorials can be gotten from amateur clubs and colleges.

Organizations such as the ARRL release study materials, other study guides may be found in local libraries. You can also practice with online test questions as some may have the exact test questions. While studying for the exam, check for the most recent version of the questions because test questions get outdated. All of these materials will further help you prepare for the examination.

Arrangements vary for different countries.

There are several classes for different licenses each having its own different package. Each of these having its own examination. Whatever the case, to be issued a license you have to pass an exam. A license class with more packages also goes along with a more difficult exam.

Wireless amateur communication is done on numerous bands (citizens band and the radio band). Some countries still require a pass in a Morse code test and also in the examination before the individual can be allowed to transmit of frequencies below 30MHz, but most countries have removed the Morse code requirement.

The more exams applicants pass, the more access they have to frequencies and other privileges. Permanent credit is given after passing a test level known as Element. The licensing exam is organized such that one is at liberty to progress at convenience.

A license is valid for a period of ten years after its issuance after which it expires. The license renewal process doesn't require passing an exam.

The types of licenses available today are the Amateur Extra, General, and the Technician.

Countries are trying to make the amateur radio hobby more attractive, so they permit those with minimal qualifications access to shortwave bands as HF and LF. However, they will not enjoy full privileges. This kind of licensing is known as Novice Licence.

License structures as stated earlier varies for different countries. In the UK, the Licencing has three structures. The first is Foundation Licence given at the entry level, Intermediate Level which has similar features with the old Novice level but operates on a higher power and a more recent Advanced Licence having all the privileges as in the

Full Licence. In some other countries, only a single license exam is available.

Try to familiarise yourself with your country's requirement. Information about this can be gotten for radio clubs.

A call sign is also issued along with a license. This unique call sign is used for station identification. It has a prefix used to identify the countries they belong.

Frequency Allocations and QSOs

Countries came together in the year 1932 to map out ways to properly regulate the growing ham radio field. Their coming together gave rise to the International Telecommunications Union (ITU). The ITU is a non-governmental forum, focused on deciding the rules that govern the usage of radio spectrum, recording and regulating all radio activities. They divided the spectrum into small ranges specific for a particular usage. These small ranges are known as *frequency allocations.*

The world has three regions, with each of these regions, have all the different radio service type. The amateur radio, commercial and military radio all have an allocation from the available frequencies. All the three regions of the world get different frequency allocations for their radio service type. But this is not the case for hams; their allocations are nearly same for all regions.

It is important that allocations like this be made especially for long distance bands where radio signals travel for a very long distance. Communicating on a different frequency is usually difficult, that is communicating with a person in another country.

Ham can communicate over different bands or frequencies allocated for their usage. The different bands are distinguished by their wavelengths; each wavelength corresponds to a particular frequency.

The bands that are mostly used are the shortwave or the high-frequency bands. They lie within 1.8MHz to 30MHz frequency range. They are also in the Very High-Frequency 144MHz.

The QSO is a code used to signify a contract made between two stations. This code helps to limit language barriers, and also reduce the characters sent in a Morse. An amateur putting out a general call or a "CQ" in search of a contact may initiate a code. When a fellow ham hears this call, he may reply and decide to exchange station details, of furthermore signal reports, and still, develop into a exchange of QSL cards and awards getting more conversational.

Hams give their cards (QSL) to establish a contact. The cards are used to confirm and claim an award for making contacts with several countries or collecting many points. Hams send QSL cards directly or in bulk. Emails to have been used to send cards.

Chapter Three
EQUIPMENT

Ham radios have graduated from the vacuum tube to sleek communication assets being controlled by microprocessors though you may find the vacuum tube radios in some stations.

The traditional radio is usually composed of a receiver and a transmitter. These two combined are referred to as the transceiver though hams call it rig. Rigs are also used to refer handheld and mobile radios.

Feedlines

Radios are usually connected to a set of antennas or a single antenna with a feedline. With the antenna switch, hams can select one of the many antennas available. Antenna exist in different forms;The dipole which usually connects to the center of the feedline and the beam antenna usually mounted on a tower having a rotator that points in different directions and can only send and receive radio waves from one direction better than others. For a very efficient transmitter operation, place an antenna in-between the feedline and the transmitter.

Feedline measurements

The Standing Wave Ratio (SWR) measures a feedline electrical condition. It also measures the amount of the transmitted power being radiated from the antenna; it is also ratio of voltages. This Standing Wave Ratio can be evaluated with antenna tuners and radios. Radios that measure and display the feedline SWR have inbuilt meters. SWR can also be measured externally with the use of a SWR meter or bridge known as stand-alone SWR sensor. This is a more convenient way of measuring SWR, especially when working on antennas and other portable conditions because it is very handy and inexpensive to get. A more accurate means of getting the SWR of a feedline is using the power meter. They measure the amount of power entering and leaving the transmitter. They are mounted at the transmitters output.

Microphones and headphones are employed for communication when transmitting speech. If you transmit with Morse code using traditional transmission device (straight keys) or more preferably use keyers and players. The paddle resembles straight keys in their pairs mounted in such a way that they lie on their sides in a back to back position. The keyer is responsible for converting the paddle levers to dashes and strings consisting of dots. Using the paddle and keyer is less stressful and faster.

Computers and other device has the ability to interpret digital data and transform them to the on-the-air signal. Sometimes, data require a multi-protocol controller for a successful processing. With the computer's serial RS-232 (COM) port, it communicates with the controller.

Filters

Filters like the name implies are used to prevent a particular range of frequencies from going through. Some filters pass or reject frequencies while others pass only specific frequencies and reject others. Filters can be made up of discrete components (which are the inductors and capacitors), from stubs a section of a feedline. Filters are of different types:

Feedline filters: feedline filters are used for preventing unwanted signals from the radio from getting to the antenna and also the other way round. They can also be used to prevent unwanted signals from the transmitter from being radiated to avoid interference with others. On transmitted signals, they can be used to ensure that unwanted signals from the transmitter are not radiated, causing interference to others. Unwanted signals can also be prevented from getting to the receiver's station with the feedline filters.

Receiving filters: Receiving filters pass only a specific signal and rejects all others in a receiver. They are made from quartz and mounted inside a radio. With this filter, you can enhance the selectivity power of your receiver increasing its ability to receive only a desired signal in the presence of other signals.

Audio: Audio filters are used to improve users output. They are mounted on the receiver output to prevent nearby signals from acting as noise.

Notch: A notch filter works to remove a very narrow range of frequencies, such as a single interfering tone.

Receivers

For tuning and listening to ham radios, one required equipment is the communications receiver. The traditional domestic radio is not efficient at receiving shortwave transmissions. Ham radio shortwave transmissions can only be received effectively using a receiver.

One of the reasons why the domestic radio is not well suitable for receiving ham radio transmissions is that they have been designed to receive high power signals and are not that sensitive to lower power ham radio stations. Their design doesn't not resolve ham radio FM transmissions because it was made for commercial broadcast transmitted on Amplitude Modulation. Only a receiver with an ability to receive Morse codes, Amplitude Modulations, and at least SSB, capable of receiving shortwave frequencies (1.8-30MHz) is capable of receiving amateur shortwave transmissions.

Transmitters / Transceivers

A transceiver is simply a combination of a transmitter and a receiver forming a single unit. It is impossible to communicate with a radio without a transceiver.

Transmitters come in different types and capabilities ranging from simple low power, low-cost transmitters that can only transmit Morse, the more common complex multipurpose high power transmitters, which can either be built from home or manufactured for commercial purposes.

Cost

A good ham radio experience doesn't cost much. Equipment for amateur radio's do not cost much.

Hams enjoy their hobby without spending too much. If you are willing to save money while you enjoy your hobby, you may consider buying surplus war equipment from government and convert it for ham radio use.

Before building radio equipment, or converting equipment to suit radio purposes, a full amateur radio license is a necessity. You may go for novice license which requires low power, low-cost equipment.

Aerials (Antennas)

Antennas do not have to be large, expensive and unsightly to be efficient. Constructing an effective shortwave antenna can be done with a simple thin flexible wire costing very little.

There are also technologies that are required in operating a ham station. This technology aids exchange of information and making of contacts using the ham radio. Some of the available technologies you will be using for your ham stations Modulation/Demodulation are listed below:

Modulation involves including information to a signal before transmitting over the air. The retrieval of the information added to a signal is known as Demodulation. Amplitude modulation (AM) and frequency modulation

(FM) are the two types of modulation we have.

Modes: Modes refers to the different ways in which added information can be sent. Voice, Morse code, data, Video, are all modes with which information can be transmitted.

Repeaters: *Repeaters* act like the relay process. They listen and transmit at the same time. Transmitting is done on a different frequency from which signals are received. With repeaters, hams can comfortably communicate over long distance with low-power radios owing to the fact that they are mounted on high platforms such as towers, hilltops, and tall buildings. They can be used for a much longer communication if they are linked together by internet or even radios. They are known for their duplex operation which involves listen and transmitting at the same time.

Satellites: hams too make use of satellite, some of its satellites function as email servers, sky repeaters as well as digital bulletin boards. Satellites are also used for commercial services as well as military.

Computer software: Computers today are no longer limited to paperwork, that involves keeping and arranging files. It is now a crucial part of the amateur radios. They regulate radio functions, create digital signals, decode them, and send Morse codes too. become a big part of ham radio.

Hams have created a means of accessing email-servers through radio. They did this by linking radio to computer networks.

Hams have also been interested in developing more advanced radio technologies. Moving away from the antiquated radios, they have created several novel radio hybrid along with other technologies. GPS radio location, internet, trying to introduce the wireless Local Area Network to ham. Several innovations are constantly going on in the world of hams, and globally members of Tucson Amateur Packet Radio (TAPR) organization are working on innovating digital methods of communication. Hams has also constructed newer antenna designs and structure. The ham world is a home to constant innovations.

Chapter four
HOW TO BECOME A RADIO AMATEUR

There are clubs that host enthusiastic, ham radio lovers who are willing to give you a the desired push in your hobby so, look out for a Nation Society of hams and try to join them or any local club. A lot of benefits accompany the joining of a National society, some of which includes exposing members to materials, tools, and trainings required to pass assessment needed before one is issued a license. If you haven't experienced the amateur radio before, then the ham club is an opportunity to get the experience. Clubs also enlighten members about the National requirements for becoming a ham. The ARRL is the national society for the USA.

Listening

For you to successfully put a contact (QSO) in your logbook, you need to learn to listen. The ham bands do not stable people, people constantly come and go every time. This is what makes your ears a valuable possession for your ham station. First, you tune the band so that you listen at different frequencies to check the ongoing activity and monitor conversations. After some time you can enter an ongoing conversation. So listening makes you discover who is presently available, their ongoing activities, and also understand the radio better. With consistent listening, you may discover a more efficient way of making contacts.

Listening on the different bands

The shortwave HF bands has a different experience from the VHF bands. Using the VHF bands, contacts can be found using repeaters and specific frequencies while on the HF bands stations are located on any frequency that offers a contact. If repeaters are not used for VHF, then channels separated by a few Kz are used. Hams hang out either on shortwave bands the high-frequency bands, Very high-frequency bands or the Ultra High-Frequency bands.

The HF bands ranges from 3 to 30 MHz; the VHF starts at 30 to 300 MHz while the UHF covers 300 MHz to 3 GHz.

Repeaters listen in one frequency and transmits in another frequency. They can transfer weak and low power signal station with their powerful transmitters over a wide distance because they are usually mounted on high platforms like towers, hilltops.

Hams activities always tends towards specific frequencies. It just happens that way, both on HF and VHF. Some low power amateur radios can be found easily on the 14.060 MHz frequency. It is not like it's the best place for them on air, but they just gather there. Cases like this makes it easier to locate contacts having like minds. These frequencies where groups gather are called the cluster frequencies. It can also be used as a source of learning new stuffs.

"Tuning in a Signal

Tuning involves changing the operating frequency of a radio with a knob. The tuning Knob is connected to the Variable Frequency Oscillator which directly controls the radio frequency. When the knob is tuned, it changes the frequency of the VFO which in turn changes the radios operating frequency. Usually, the radios operating signal frequency is displayed on the dial, but this only displays when tuning is done properly. The right way to tune is dependent on the signal type to be received. Tuning with the ears work well for signals such as the FM or Morse codes which are copied manually. Tuning can be done from the displays for signals which require using special equipment such as PSK31, packet, and RTTY. To be sent. Tuning to a frequency can be done from either directly above the signal and below, but with time you can decide which one is more preferred.

Choose your preferred radio type and set your radio to either USB, Morse, FM or AM. Allow all signals to pass by putting off the squelch control. The job of the squelch control when it is on is to silence the audio until there is an available signal. But if it is put off temporarily, the weakest signal can be easily heard on its entering.

Morse code (CW)

Another wave for the Morse code is Continuous wave. Early hams had issues with radio signals because they fade easily. Sparks were used to generate these signal, so they weren't consistent. With time they developed more advanced way of generating steady signals because they were steady and continuous they were termed the Continuous wave (CW). Since then, the term Morse code and Continuous wave have been used interchangeably. The Telegraph is used to control the Continuous waves; you can decide to either turn it on or off.

Follow the steps below to tune in to a Continuous wave or Morse code signal:

1. From the rig settings, select CW mode to start receiving Morse code.

2. If you have several filters mounted on your rig, select the wider filter in the rig set-up.

It is better to use a wider filter to allow all the available signals both far and near to pass freely. With the wider filter, you can easily find stations and tune in to them. Narrow filters prevents nearby signals from passing through. Each of the filters are have switches or controls that carry the filters width. You can also check the operating manual that come with the filters for instructions on how the filter works.

3. Continue the tuning the dial until a Morse code signal is in range.

Each frequency goes with its own pitch. Some frequencies have pitches that are very loud and clear while others have moderate pitches. Do not stop tuning until you find a pitch that is comfortable for your ears that is not too loud and not too low. Frequencies within the range of 300-600Hz are low pitch which are very restful to the ear while frequencies within the range of 500–1200 Hz are louder and clearer. When making a contact and your radio is tuned to a frequency of about 500Hz with a particular tone and pitch, the transmitted signal is also received at the same frequency, tone, and pitch. If you are not comfortable with the pitch that comes along with the frequency you tuned in to, you can adjust the rig settings to suit your preferred tone and pitch. The process of adjusting pitch is stated in your rigs operating manual.

4. When you are done with tuning and have selected the pitch of your choice, select the narrower filter to limit noise and interference of signals.

Subsequently, as you garner experience in the use of ham radios, you will discover other practical ways to use your hobby. Your hobby can be turned into service for the benefit of the people around you. Amateur radios also have the service part that can also be rendered.

The amateur service render services such as making available emergency communication devices, providing efficient and trained operators in return for the privileges that comes with getting licensed. After the licensing, hams are free to access a wide range of frequencies; they are protected from noise and other forms interference. Forms of interference, maintenance of technical standards, and enforcement of operating rules. Apart from emergency functions, hams can also be used to get information about weather, for communications at social and public functions and also provide tutorials for interested amateur radio operators. Their message handling is very effective for emergency and ordinary events because it is always available at any time. However, this step can be overlooked if the frequency is not crowded.

Other sections you can fit in as an amateur radio operator is listed below;

Assistant Section Manager (ASM): You can be an assistant to the already appointed section manager. You job will be to assist the manager in tasks accorded to the office such as collecting reports, analyzing volunteer reports, scrutinizing the reports from local and regional nets. Each section has its own duties. Sometimes some tasks may arise, and your assistance would be needed to carry it out.

Official Emergency Stations (OES): The local emergency coordinators direct the activities of this section. You have to perform all the duties assigned to you by your coordinators. The appointments give room for participating in projects. You will also have the opportunity to be part of the different teams such as operation, logistics, and administration. They are given to emcomm duties.

Public Information Officer (PIO): Serving as a public relation officers, you will create new relationships with the media houses both regional and local. Relationships between community leaders and organizations will also be created as most of the public services rendered by hams will require the assistance of several organizations. This is because ham radio reports are publicized with the media. They publicize reports on the public services and other emcomm performed for the public.

Official Observer (OO): Official Observers are out to identify unlicensed transmissions, irregularities on a frequency. They look out for unlicensed amateur radio operators and prevent them from violating the Federal Communications Commission's rules.

Technical Specialist (TS): If you are well experienced in a specific radio operations you can play the role of a Technical specialist. You can also be a consultant in the national society for hams in your country, to the local hams as well as regional hams or for any hams club. As a technical specialist, you can also organize training sessions to assist upcoming hams.

CONCLUSION

Thank you again for purchasing this book!

I hope this book was able to help you to get your Ham Radio and obtaining the license.

The next step is to bring all you have learned into reality.

Finally, if you enjoyed this book, then I'd like to ask you for a favor, would you be kind enough to leave a review for this book on Amazon? It'd be greatly appreciated!

Thank you and good luck!

www.ingramcontent.com/pod-product-compliance
Lightning Source LLC
Chambersburg PA
CBHW070950180426
43194CB00041B/2035